MAKING SENSE OF BEHAVIOUR

SUPPORTING PUPILS WITH EMOTIONAL
AND BEHAVIOURAL DIFFICULTIES
THROUGH CONSISTENCY

by

Rob Long

A NASEN PUBLICATION

ISBN 1 901485 14 5

Published by NASEN.
NASEN is a company limited by guarantee, registered in England and Wales. Company No. 2674379.
NASEN is a registered charity. Charity No. 1007023.

Further copies of this book and details of NASEN's many other publications may be obtained from the Publications Department at its registered office: NASEN House, 4/5 Amber Business Village, Amber Close, Amington, Tamworth, Staffs. B77 4RP.
Tel: 01827 311500; Fax: 01827 313005
Email: welcome@nasen.org.uk; Website: www.nasen.org.uk

Cover design by Raphael Creative Design.
Typeset in Times by J. C. Typesetting and printed in the United Kingdom by Stowes (Stoke-on-Trent).

Contents

Preface   4

Introduction   5

Child Development   7

The Consistency Model   11

Guidelines for Applying Sanctions   14

Promoting Positive Behaviours   16

Guidelines for Applying Rewards   17

Appendixes   20

Preface

Supporting Pupils with Emotional and Behavioural Difficulties through Consistency is one of eight booklets in the series *Making Sense of Behaviour* by Rob Long. The others are *Exercising Self-control; Developing Self-esteem through Positive Entrapment for Pupils facing Emotional and Behavioural Difficulties; Friendships; Understanding and Supporting Depressed Children and Young People; Not Me, Miss! The Truth about Children who Lie; Challenging Confrontation: Information and Techniques for School Staff;* and *Learning to Wave: Some Everyday Guidelines for Stress Management.*

Challenging Confrontation gives information and techniques for teachers to use when dealing with argumentative, angry and difficult pupils. *Supporting Pupils with Emotional and Behavioural Difficulties through Consistency* advocates a whole-school approach for low-level misbehaviours whilst *Learning to Wave* is written for teachers themselves. It contains advice about coping with the stress which might arise from dealing with children with behavioural problems.

The other five titles give practical ideas and information for teachers to use with children with worrying behaviours in their classes. These are written to help teachers both understand and change some of the difficulties that children might experience (depression, lack of self-control, low self-esteem, friendship problems and lying).

Each book stands alone but when read as a set the behavioural issues and their solutions overlap and this emphasises the need for positive and consistent strategies to be put into place throughout the school.

Acknowledgements
The author and publishers wish to express their grateful thanks to Lorna Johnston, Agnes Donnelly and Dorothy Smith for their helpful suggestions and comments.

Supporting Pupils with Emotional and Behavioural Difficulties through Consistency

Introduction

In large primary schools and all secondary schools the task of consistently managing students' behaviour successfully is a constant challenge. While more and more schools are successfully developing in-school strategies to support the more challenging students, in-class support for everyday misdemeanours is usually minimum. These usually include behaviours such as:

- out of seat;
- no equipment;
- answering back;
- not listening;
- homework not completed;
- attention seeking.

More often it is these low-level misbehaviours which are most disruptive and stressful to teachers. It is so easy for a well-planned lesson to become less than successful when teachers are faced by students who seem determined to interrupt, distract and disagree. This booklet has two main objectives:

1. To develop a Consistency Model that enables a whole-school approach to in-class misbehaviour.
2. To develop a Consistency Model that enables a whole-school approach to positive behaviours.

The consistent use of both rewards and sanctions are the keys to successful classroom management. Our aim is to teach students that when they behave and follow the rules, they will earn a range of positive outcomes. We must be clear in our own minds that we reward students because of what they do; that is, they *earn* the rewards. The same applies to sanctions. Inappropriate behaviours result in outcomes that students do not like. Appropriately used rewards and sanctions can teach students that they can control their behaviour and determine what the outcomes will be.

The need for consistency

At the heart of any whole-school approach to behaviour management is consistency - the need for all staff to respond in similar ways to similar behaviours.

This:

- shows students that similar behaviours are treated the same by different teachers;
- removes the pressure on staff to decide how best to respond to a wide range of behaviours.

Positive behaviour consistently rewarded will be increased, while inappropriate behaviour that is consistently sanctioned will decrease. (If these principles were understood by students life would be a lot easier!)

A major reason why consistency is difficult to achieve is that a behaviour policy may be imposed on staff. This can result in staff making their own sense of how they should apply the policy. Every school has its own history and unique ethos which exist within the daily routines and rituals. Consistency can best be achieved when all staff participate in deciding and agreeing on how they will manage students' behaviour.

We know that students want to be treated consistently. All students have a strong sense of fairness. They quickly notice and resent what they consider to be unfair and inconsistent treatment. For a teacher this is not always easy. When, for example, a usually well-behaved student misbehaves it can be too easy to overlook it, but we need to respond as we would to any other student who misbehaves.

To achieve consistency we need to involve all staff and draw together the existing methods that are used to manage student behaviour. Every successful school knows that behaviour is always a management issue. The more successfully behaviour is managed, the more teaching and learning takes place. Students will always explore the boundaries of their behaviour and in so doing learn what is acceptable and what is not. All schools need to decide how it will promote positive behaviours and sanction inappropriate ones.

Child Development

Before presenting the Consistency Model in detail it is important that some consideration is given to the pupils/students we have in our school. From child studies we are aware of the different stages children pass through on their journey towards adulthood. Any whole-school approach to behaviour management should reflect the stages of development of its children. It is no good developing a behaviour policy that ignores the children.

While we want our children to take responsibility for their actions it is pointless to act as if they are capable of this when they are not. While age acts as a rough indicator of what we expect children of different ages to be able to do, there is considerable variation within any age group. Within a class there are likely to be children who follow the class rules because:

- 'Might is right' - they do what is expected of them because they are children and we are adults. This approach is *directive* and is teacher centred.
- There will also be some children who follow the rules because of the consequences - they like the rewards. This is the *behavioural approach* and is still predominantly teacher centred.
- There will also be some children who follow the rules because they know that they make sense, that it helps them to live together as a community. This approach is *pupil centred* and involves teachers much less.

As you can see in the figure below, the more children are at stage 1 the more active and interventionist is the role of the adult. While at stage 3 the adults' role is greatly diminished. We clearly want to move children towards stage 3, but our behaviour management approaches must take these points into account.

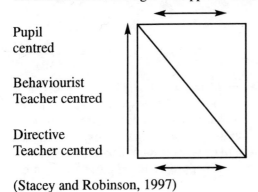

Pupil
centred

Behaviourist
Teacher centred

Directive
Teacher centred

(Stacey and Robinson, 1997)

7

In reality our behaviour plans will encompass a little from each approach but more from some stages. Infant children will be directed more by teachers, but their teachers will be encouraging the children to make decisions for themselves wherever possible. Similarly not every adolescent will be thinking abstractly; many will prefer concrete examples, and rewards are as important to the 13 year-old as the 5 year-old. There will, at times, be adolescents who are emotionally no older than 6 years as they struggle to cope with frustrations.

Rewards are important at each stage, but ideally, rewards will become more internalised as a child matures. The more mature the student, the less dependent s/he is likely to be on external rewards. At this stage children will be capable of holding in their mind their own idea of how they see themselves and compare this to the standards of others that are important to them. If children are not helped and encouraged to internally reward themselves they can become over-reliant on praise and other forms of rewards and find it difficult to judge for themselves how well they have done.

The Developmental Wheel
It will be helpful before proceeding to develop the Consistency Model if we briefly remind ourselves of the characteristics of the pupils/students in our school. Each spoke of the wheel reflects a key aspect of development that is central to children and young people learning to take control of their behaviour.

1. Conflict
2. Frustration
3. Delayed Gratification
4. Cognitive
5. Social Skills
6. Friendships

While you will be thinking of the school as a whole and looking for typical answers, you may at a later date wish to use it with a specific student in mind. It can help focus on areas of development that can explain some of the emotional and behavioural difficulties a student may be experiencing. If, for whatever reason, one of the spokes is short then the student is more than likely to have a "bumpy" ride unless appropriate support systems are put in place.

When you know a child well you will be able to decide quite quickly which area needs support and development. The questions presented below are examples of the skills children master to enable them to cope successfully with everyday school life - a particular skill. If they have not mastered them, then they are likely to experience difficulties. As you can see it is possible to visually present how well you believe a child has mastered the key skills.

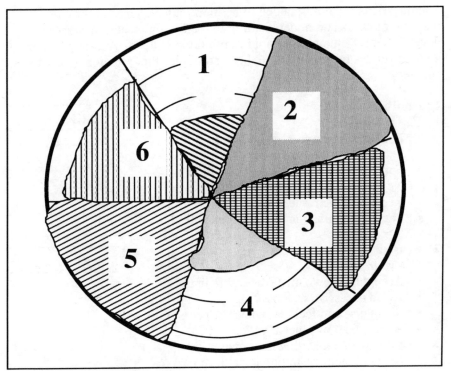

The Developmental Wheel

Indicative Questions
The developmental profile will point to the management strategies you
may use. These questions will highlight where students are in relation to
the skills. In scoring the questions each is given a value of 1. Infants will be
doing well if they score around 12. There may be many secondary students
who may achieve a score of 30, on a "good day", while junior age children
can be expected to score around 24.

The questions are not intended to be hierarchical. They are pointers to
the kind of skills and understanding that children master during their
development. Remember to hold in mind the skills of your pupils and
students to ensure that you use those strategies that are most likely to
succeed.

1. Conflict
Can your pupils:

SCORE ....

- Find an adult to sort out conflicts?
- Stand up for their rights?
- Forgive other people if they hurt them?
- Negotiate and compromise?
- Recognise their role in disputes?
- Show determination to resolve disputes?

2. Frustration
Can your pupils:

SCORE ....

- Accept their own mistakes and failings?
- Avoid excessive jealousy?
- Recognise and feel fear when danger is present?
- Accept their own negative feelings?
- Cope with not getting their own way?
- Channel their frustration to achieve goals?

3. Delayed Gratification
Can your pupils:

SCORE ....

- Understand short and long periods of time?
- Be honest, even when it is difficult?
- Stop doing something enjoyable when asked?
- Plan and work to long-term goals?
- Persist at set tasks to succeed?
- Work for short periods for an agreed reward?

4. Cognitive Aspects

SCORE ....

Can your pupils:
- Recognise and label their own feelings?
- Use language to conceptualise the world?
- Define a problem, find solutions and choose a solution?
- Let thoughts mediate between events and action?
- Imagine the world as other people see it?
- Think abstractly and hypothetically?

5. Social Skills

SCORE ....

Can your pupils:
- Share and take turns?
- Discuss common interests with adults and peers?
- Give support and help to others?
- Begin and end conversations?
- Show positive feelings towards others?
- Reveal personal information appropriately?

6. Friendships

SCORE ....

Can your pupils:
- Empathise with peers who have been hurt?
- Explain the role of listening, helping and caring?
- Enjoy playing alongside each other?
- Meet new peers and start a conversation?
- Actively make efforts to include isolates?
- Enjoy and seek out opposite sex peers?

See Appendix for profile chart.

The Consistency Model

The model presented below is neither complicated nor highly theoretical. It is what all schools know they should do, but have never found the time to do it. Often schools can pay consultants to come in and tell them how to be consistent, little realising that they were sitting on the answer themselves. This approach is based on:

1. *All* staff meeting together to construct their own Consistent Behaviour Management Plan.
2. Jig-saws, as a group technique.

The Model

To be consistent *all* teachers need to have a range of recommended strategies for dealing with misbehaviours. For example, if a student shouts out inappropriately, then the teacher uses one of a range of recommended actions. This is helpful to individual teachers as they do not have to constantly think and decide what is best to do. It is good for the student because they will experience similar responses from different teachers.

The Consistency Model makes explicit good practice that is already taking place in a school. It enables each teacher to look at common concerns through a "template" that has been constructed by the whole school. It does not say, "you must use these strategies", it says, "these are the ways in which your colleagues suggest you manage such and such a behaviour". A possible limitation with this model is that it is possible for a range of inappropriate techniques to become standard practice. To limit this, it is recommended that staff measure strategies against the following criteria.

1. Does the strategy take into account the student's level of development and understanding?
2. Does the strategy promote understanding and self-control within the student?
3. Does the strategy deal with the behaviour firmly, while treating the student with respect?
4. Are there ways of increasing desired behaviour as well as reducing undesirable behaviour?
5. Is the student involved in setting behaviour targets?
6. Are there good links between school, home and the student?
7. Do the strategies aim to promote or develop understanding and empathy with regard to the student's difficulties?

The Jig-saw Technique

Jig-saws is a very flexible and creative way for groups to work together. The best way to explain it is to describe it being used by a whole school to develop consistent ways of dealing with the five most common in-class behavioural difficulties met by teachers. Every school will naturally produce a different model (see worked example on next page).

School size: 50 staff plus 1 coordinator task. To produce in-class strategies for common misbehaviour.

Step 1   Create ten mixed groups of five.

Step 2   Each group discusses the main concerns and writes each one on a Post-it note.

Step 3   Coordinator collects these and places them on a flip chart and clusters similar concerns together.

Step 4   The top five concerns are chosen and a colour is allocated to each one.

Step 5   In each group a coloured piece of A4 is given to each member. The concern that matches that colour is written on it.

Step 6   Groups are now given five minutes on each concern to discuss strategies for dealing with each concern. The person who has the concern that is being discussed takes notes of all the ideas suggested.

Step 7   New groups are now formed - expert groups - with all the yellows joining together and all the reds etc.

Step 8   Each expert group, five in total, now has 15 minutes to share all the ideas that were produced on any one of the five concerns. Common ideas are looked for. The group then produces a list of the top five most frequently recommended and successful strategies (bearing in mind the Indicative Questions on pages 10 and 11 and the criteria on page 12). These are not numbered as they are *not* necessarily hierarchical.

A member from each of the expert groups then feeds back to the whole group their list of five top recommendations for the concern. These lists are collected and summarised on one sheet which is distributed to all members of staff. On the next page is an example. (Also see Appendix 1 for a further example.)

SHOUTING OUT	ATTENTION SEEKING	NO EQUIPMENT
Frequently remind student of rule	Ignore	Reminder given and record kept
Ask and praise student who has hand up	Reward success	Provide back-up set
Catch them following the rule	Sit them with a model student	Student reports daily with equipment
Record progress and set target and discuss with student	Set targets	Acronym designed as reminder
Pair with student who follows the rule	Payback system, remain behind at end of lesson	Agreed rewards provided

THE CONSISTENCY MODEL

NO HOMEWORK	GUIDELINES	LATENESS
Explain consequences	**CLASSROOM BEHAVIOUR IS ALWAYS A MANAGEMENT ISSUE FOR YOU**	Special late chair provided
Support arranged		Discuss at end of lesson
Check that there is no learning difficulty	Use these strategies when appropriate for each of the above difficulties. The more students are managed in similar ways the more effective your efforts will be.	Pair with punctual peer
Student writes letter to parents		Contract for being on time agreed
Detention given		Time and work is made up

Example of Jig-saw Technique.

Guidelines for Applying Sanctions

"It ain't what you do"

How a sanction is applied can be as important as *which* sanction is applied. Sanctions can be used in such a way as to help a student learn appropriate behaviour. Even the tone of voice can convey how much conviction we have about the sanction. Below are some guidelines and tips that can increase a teacher's effectiveness when using sanctions.

1. Check understanding. If you ask a child whether they agree with a course of action you have suggested, most will say, "yes". Instead, ask them to tell you what it is that they have agreed to do.
2. If a student seems to be "playing to the audience", deal with them just outside the room.
3. Convey to a student that you have high expectations of them and are disappointed when they let themselves down.

14

4. When a student misbehaves ask them to explain to you the rule that they are not following.
5. Emphasise to a student that it is their behaviour that is earning them the sanction. If they do not like what it is earning then they need to change how they are behaving.
6. Remind students that they are responsible for their behaviour. Sometimes they make poor choices. This is usually because they have not *stopped* and *thought* whether they were about to make a *good choice* or a *bad choice*.
7. Avoid being "hijacked" especially by older students. Keep to the issue at hand, and don't get drawn into making such comments as, "Look at me when I'm talking to you." This will distract you from the issue at hand.
8. To stay calm, remember to delay immediate responses when you are becoming annoyed. "I'm going to take a few minutes while I decide how best to deal with that behaviour."
9. It is not the size of the sanction that always matters. For example being made to wait a few minutes until the rest of the class has left can be ignominious for a student who seeks peer approval.
10. Make it clear to a student that once an incident has been dealt with then as far as you are concerned it is finished. You expect normal relations to be re-established.
11. Avoid making threats and not carrying them out. This will only teach your students that they may get away with misbehaviours.
12. Maintain a professional distance with students. Over-familiarity as a means of managing problem behaviour rarely works. Being supportive and caring is different from handing complete control over to a student.
13. The closer the sanction is in time to the misdemeanour the more effective it is likely to be.
14. Avoid at all costs sanctions aimed at the student rather than the behaviour. Sarcasm, embarrassment, fear etc. will worsen matters rather than help them. Ask yourself how you would feel if you were in the same situation.
15. Use "management by walkabout". This will enable you to nip many problems in the bud. Standing next to a student who is not attending or who is disrupting others can produce the desired effect without interrupting the lesson flow.
16. Within your Consistency Model, use variety in how you deliver sanctions. A letter to a student describing their misbehaviour, the rule broken and the need for an agreed improvement can produce more results than a "good talking too". Finish the letter just with your name rather than "Yours Sincerely".

Promoting Positive Behaviours

Having addressed misbehaviours we need now to produce a similar approach to positive behaviours. Again we will use the jig-saw approach. This time, however, we will look at the different strands that contribute to a school's ways of supporting, encouraging and rewarding appropriate behaviour. Sometimes appropriate behaviour such as attending, listening, persevering, planning, cooperating, sharing and supporting will be reflected in completed work. These strands are presented in the figure below.

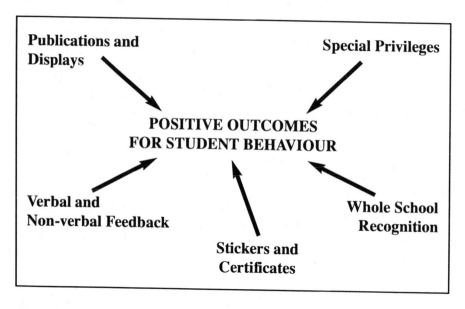

These will, of course, exist in a school, but how many of us either forget or come to rely on a narrow selection of rewards? The Consistency Model can help remind staff of the wide range of techniques for positively supporting students. It is not uncommon for staff to discover new ideas as they share their ideas with each other. The Consistency Model is not intended to stifle creativity but to share and promote the good practice that is at the core of all successful schools. While most staff will be fully aware of how their school rewards students, this can be a useful aide-memoir. With the best will in the world we all sometimes forget good practice.

PUBLICATIONS AND DISPLAYS	SPECIAL PRIVILEGES	WHOLE-SCHOOL RECOGNITION
Use Notice Boards Special Celebration Board for extra curricula activities Contact local press and radio Exhibitions in local library Concerts and performances	Peer Mentor School Council Classroom duties Charity work Choice of activities	Plays School magazine Recognition by Senior Staff Assembly Awards TV/radio press

THE CONSISTENCY MODEL

STICKERS AND CERTIFICATES	POSITIVE CONSEQUENCES GUIDELINES	VERBAL AND NON-VERBAL FEEDBACK
Certificates of attendance Handwritten comments Letters home Specific subject award Student of month	Students of *all* ages enjoy a wide range of rewards. Research suggests a ratio of 4:1 rewards for each negative in a lesson. Use this sheet to remind yourself of the different ways of letting your students know that you are impressed with their efforts and achievements.	Smile/eye contact/ sticker/material reward Comments and grades on work Showing work to class Class applause Personal praise and attention

Example of strategies for positive behaviour.

Guidelines for Applying Rewards

Because we are focusing on behaviour, some people question why we should reward behaviour that we expect from all children. "If I reward one child for staying in their seat, shouldn't I reward them all?" For many children we need to produce a differentiated behavioural curriculum. We can no longer assume that all children enter school with the same basic social skills that we are used to. They may need to be taught the skills of sharing, turn-taking, listening, cooperating etc. But they, just as their peers who face physical or sensory challenges, have the same right to be supported and included.

1. Praise and rewards are the best ways of highlighting appropriate behaviour to both young children and adolescents - "Catch them being good and reward them."
2. Rewards are only rewarding if students are motivated to work for them. Use a variety of different rewards. Have some surprises.

3. Involve students in deciding the goals they wish to achieve and the kinds of rewards they would like to have.
4. Remember rewards are not bribes. A bribe is something given to induce someone to act illegally or immorally.
5. Give lots of small rewards to a student who is just learning a new skill.
6. There are many different kinds of rewards.

   Tangible (sweets and stickers)
   - Token rewards such as stickers that can be converted into something else.

   Preferred activities
   - Social rewards such as praise and approval.
   - Intrinsic rewards are the feeling of success and pride that a student experiences.

   Work with the rewards that a child enjoys having, while pairing them with the rewards at the next level. "Here's a sticker for that piece of work, I am so impressed with the effort you put into it." The blind and inappropriate use of rewards can have a negative impact on how children learn the intrinsic satisfaction of learning.
7. Rewards can indicate that a student is succeeding and promote confidence. But be aware of students who become over-reliant and attention seeking.
8. Set the student the task of noticing small improvements that show that things are getting better. This may be short periods of free time when they related well with their peers.
9. Always find a student's "brilliant corner" and develop it.
10. Promote class teamwork by celebrating whole-class successes as well as the whole class celebrating the success of an individual.
11. Keep a record of student or class progress and remind them of how far they have come, where they were and where they are.
12. No matter what happens, a reward earned should not be taken back for later misbehaviour.
13. Keep a record of how well you are rewarding your class, and reward yourself if you meet your target. Try the record sheet in the figure below as a quick visual reference.

Once a Consistency Model has been produced for five common classroom misdemeanours, it is not the end. At a later date new ones might need to be considered. This approach could also usefully be used to tackle some of the difficulties and issues to do with free time. A blank form (Appendix 2) is included.

Ideally The Consistency Model for positive and negative behaviours would be issued on a single, laminated sheet to each member of staff to be used as an aide-memoir throughout the term. It could prove to be of great value as a quick reference for new members of staff as well as supply teachers.

TERM .... DATE .... STUDENTS' NAMES							
Rewards							
Merits							
Certificates							
Work Displayed							
Special Positions							
School Events							

Record of rewards.

ANSWERING BACK	ATTENTION SEEKING	DISTRACTING OTHERS
Ignore	Ignore	Use non-verbal reminder
Log name in book and discuss at end of lesson	Set targets	Verbally remind student of the rule
Sit with a polite student	Catch them doing well	Set written work and talk to student later
Set tasks that allow student to "bin the sin"	Have a range of rewards	Change seating arrangements or groupings
Catch them being good with a range of rewards	Set payback system, they miss playtime	Teach whole class to be quiet before end of lesson

THE CONSISTENCY MODEL

DISTRACTING SELF	GUIDELINES	INAPPROPRIATE LANGUAGE
Start with clear desk	**CLASSROOM BEHAVIOUR IS ALWAYS A MANAGEMENT ISSUE FOR YOU**	Extend vocabulary
Direct through alternative task, fold arms		Isolate from friends
Discuss with individual	Use these strategies when appropriate for each of the above difficulties. The more students are managed in similar ways the more effective will be your efforts.	Talk with student at lesson end about context
Use range of rewards		Teach student to STOP, THINK then SPEAK
Confiscate equipment		Find student's "brilliant corner" - self-esteem

Appendix 1.

THE CONSISTENCY MODEL

GUIDELINES

Appendix 2.

The Developmental Wheel

Shade in scores achieved in each section. This will clearly indicate at an individual level those skills that perhaps need developing in a pupil to enable them to make progress through their school life given the different expectations that exist at different phases.

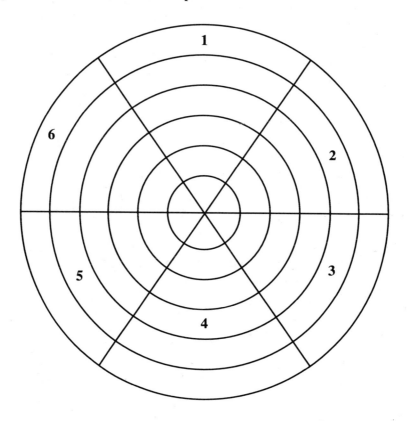

References

Creemers, B. (1994) *The Effective Classroom*, Cassell: London.

Fogell, J. & Long, R. (1997) *Spotlight on Special Educational Needs: Emotional and Behavioural Difficulties*, NASEN: Tamworth.

McPhillimy, B. (1996) *Controlling Your Class*, Wiley: Chichester.

Robertson, J. (1989) *Effective Classroom Control*, Hodder & Stoughton: London.

Stacey, H. & Robinson, P. (1997) *Let's Mediate*, Lucky Duck Publishing: Bristol.

Strayhorn, J. M. (1988) *The Competent Child*. The Guilford Press: New York.